EQUESTRIAN EVENTS

A TRUE BOOK

by

Bob Knotts

Children's Press®
A Division of Grolier Publishing
New York London Hong Kong Sydney
Danbury, Connecticut

Reading Consultant
Linda Cornwell
*Coordinator of School Quality
and Professional Improvement
Indiana State Teachers
Association*

Author's Dedication:
*To Jill,
my favorite show jumper.*

Participant in a
three-day event

Visit Children's Press® on the
Internet at:
http://publishing.grolier.com

Library of Congress Cataloging-in-Publication Data

Knotts, Bob.
    Equestrian events / by Bob Knotts
        p.   cm. — (A true book)
    Includes bibliographical references and index.
    Summary: Describes the connection between horses and people,
show jumping, dressage, and various equestrian events.
    ISBN 0-516-21062-9 (lib. bdg.)   0-516-27025-7 (pbk.)
    1. Horse sports Juvenile literature. [1. Horse sports. 2. Horses.
3. Horsemanship.] I. Title. II. Series.
    SF294.23.K56   2000
    798.2'4—dc21
                                                                                99-27881
                                                                                CIP
                                                                                AC

GROLIER
PUBLISHING

Contents

Horses and People

Many people love horses. Maybe you love horses, too. Horses are strong and sleek. They are beautiful animals to watch. They are usually tame enough that you can pet and feed them. People enjoy watching horses run and play and shake their heads and swish their tails.

5

Riders sit on a saddle and use reins to control the horse.

Lots of people love to ride horses, too. Riders sit on a saddle, a leather seat strapped to the horse's back. Riders also hold reins—leather straps attached to a horse's mouth. Riders use the reins to help tell a horse what to do.

Have you ever had a chance to ride a horse? If so, you're very lucky. It's exciting to feel such a powerful animal under you. And it's fun to learn how to control a horse—how to

A young rider jumping a fence

make a horse go and stop and turn. You must also learn how to make a horse speed up and slow down on your command. This takes practice, and it's only the beginning of what horses and people can do together.

Sometimes people ride horses in difficult competitions. These competitions are called equestrian events. "Equestrian" is a word that describes any activity that has

Show jumping is one type
of equestrian event.

to do with horseback riding.
So equestrian events are
horseback-riding events. The
word "equestrian" comes
from *equus,* the Latin word
for "horse."

Equestrian events can be
fun to watch. They are exciting

Equestrian events are exciting to watch.

and beautiful. Sometimes they are dangerous, though. They require lots of training—for both the riders and the horses.

Expert riders can teach their horses to jump over things. This is called show jumping.

Some horses learn to make special, beautiful movements of their legs that look like dancing. This is called dressage. Other horses are trained to do all of this, as well as to run

Show jumping (left) and dressage (below)

The second day of
a three-day event

quickly over trails and through woods. This is called three-day eventing.

Show jumping, dressage, and three-day eventing are part of the Summer Olympic Games. Each of these events have both individual and team competitions. Many riders and horses from around the world compete every four years in the Olympics. Those who win gold medals—the Olympic prize for first place—are known as the best in their sport.

Gold, silver, and bronze Olympic medalists in team dressage

Horseback

Ancient Greek drawing of a chariot race

Ancient Roman chariot race

Horseback-riding competitions are at least 6,500 years old. The ancient Sumerians were among the first people to hold such contests. Equestrian events, including chariot races,

History

were part of the ancient Olympics in Greece. Chariot racing was also a very popular sport in ancient Rome.

In the 1500s, wealthy men in Europe became interested in horseback riding. They began to hold competitions to see who was best.

One modern event, show jumping, may have started in Paris in 1866. By 1900, equestrian events were included in the modern Olympic Games.

A three-day event in the 1940s

Show Jumping

It is hard enough for most people just to *ride* a horse. So imagine riding a horse that jumps over fences more than 5 1/2 feet (1.7 m) high! That's what riders in show jumping do. Their horses must jump over fifteen to twenty obstacles, usually fences.

In show jumping, horse and rider leap over tall obstacles.

Sometimes the horses also jump over water, or over a triple bar—three fences right in a row. The rider tries to guide the horse over the obstacles

Show jumpers must sometimes leap over a water jump (above) or a triple combination— three fences right in a row (left).

so that the horse's legs or feet don't knock down any part of the fence. Competitors get faults, or penalty points, if the horse knocks down a fence.

Faults are also given if a horse refuses to jump, falls, or jumps the obstacles in the wrong order. At each competition, the course, or series of jumps, is different. The rider is allowed to walk the course

Faults are given if the horse falls or refuses to jump.

WHITBREA

Riders are allowed to walk the course before the event begins.

before mounting the horse. The horse, however, sees the jumps for the first time during the competition.

A clock is ticking as the horse moves over the course. Faults are given if the horse takes too much time to finish the course. This means that each rider must try to get the horse to move just fast enough. A horse that moves too fast may knock down fences and receive faults. But a horse that moves too slowly will also receive faults.

The horse and rider work together as a team.

The trick for the rider is to know how fast is too fast— and how slow is too slow. So the rider must understand the horse very well. And riders must know how to get the best from their horses.

Show jumping and other equestrian events are unusual in one important way. Men and women can compete against each other in these sports. This is true whether the competition is a small event or the Olympic Games.

An unusual view of a horse and rider crossing a water jump

A rider must be at least eighteen years old to enter show jumping or three-day eventing in the Olympics. Riders in dressage must be at least sixteen years old. Even the horses must be old enough to compete—at least seven years old!

Dressage

In all equestrian events, it's important that the rider and the horse work together as a team. They must respect and care about each other. This is especially true in dressage. A dressage horse must instantly obey every command of the rider.

24

In dressage, horses perform precision movements.

Dressage requires horses to perform movements they would not make without years of training. In fact, the word *dressage* comes from the French word for "training." As judges watch, the horse and

rider enter the arena where the competition takes place. They walk together to the first of twelve markers, or small signs.

At the first marker, the horse must do certain movements that show how well it is trained.

These movements are a type of test. Then the horse and rider move on to the next marker—and to the next test. The judges give scores from zero to ten for each movement the horse makes. The rider also is judged. The horse and rider that show the best training as a team will win.

Some of the movements the horse makes are some-what simple. For example, the horse must stop squarely with its front and back feet even. But other movements

A square halt

A horse beginning a pirouette

are very difficult. One of these is called the pirouette. In the pirouette, the horse must turn in a circle by moving its feet as if it were dancing.

Freestyle dressage is another event. Freestyle dressage requires that horses and riders

perform to music. In this type of dressage, the horses look very much like they are dancing.

In the Olympics, dressage is made up of three rounds. The first two rounds are set routines and the third round is freestyle.

A Brave Rider Becomes a Champion

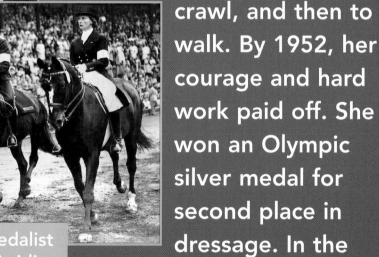

Lis Hartel with her horse "Jubilee"

In 1944, Lis Hartel was one of Denmark's best riders. Then, she became seriously ill with polio, a disease that can paralyze people. Lis couldn't move. But Lis gradually taught herself to lift her arm, then to crawl, and then to walk. By 1952, her courage and hard work paid off. She won an Olympic silver medal for second place in dressage. In the 1956 Olympics, she won another silver medal. Hartel is a true Olympic hero.

Olympic silver medalist Lis Hartel (at left) riding alongside the 1956 gold and bronze medalists in dressage

Three-Day Eventing

Three-day eventing is the most difficult Olympic event for horses and riders. As its name suggests, this event takes place over three days.

On the first day, the horses and riders compete in dressage. The second day, called the cross-country phase, is

The cross-country phase of a three-day event

the hardest. The competitors must run in four races over roads, tracks, and trails. On the third day, the horses and riders take part in show jumping.

The races on the second day are very tiring—and sometimes dangerous. The

The show-jumping phase of a three-day event

Three-day events are tiring and sometimes dangerous.

horses must run long distances. In one race, they must jump over logs, water, ditches, and stone walls. Three horses died in three-day eventing during

A veterinarian checking a horse during a three-day event

the 1936 Olympics in Berlin, Germany. But today, veterinarians, or animal doctors, check the horses during competition.

Three-day eventing comes from the military. It shows how horses were trained for the army many years ago. The horses had to look good on parade. They also had to have the strength, courage, and ability to keep going after long runs. Only army officers riding military horses were allowed to compete when three-day eventing was first included in the Olympics.

Other Equestrian Events

Some equestrian events not included in the Olympic Games are part of other important competitions.

One of these events is endurance riding. This requires the horses and riders to run over very long trails—much

Endurance riding
in Algeria

longer than those in three-day
eventing. The trails are often
50 miles (80 km) long!

Another event is called
combined driving. In this
event, riders sit in a cart or

Combined driving

carriage and drive the horse
from behind. The horse pulls
the cart and driver. These
teams compete in tests
designed to show how strong
and well-trained the horses are.

Reining is another equestrian event. Reining shows the athletic abilities of ranch horses. In this event, the horses are required to make the movements that horses make when they are rounding up cattle. In a reining competition, the horses must run fast and then quickly change direction. They also must run in circles, walk backwards, and make many other moves that require lots of training.

It is hard to become an expert rider, and it is even harder to train a horse to take part in competition. Such training requires skill and knowledge of horses, as well as patience and hard work. Those who make it all the way to the Olympic Games aren't just lucky. They have dreamed for years about competing in the Olympics. And they have tried very hard to make that dream come true for themselves and the horses they love.

Becoming an expert rider takes a lot of time and practice.

To Find Out More

Here are some additional resources to help you learn more about equestrian events:

 **Books**

Condon, Robert J. **Great Women Athletes of the Twentieth Century.** McFarland, 1991.

Evans, Jeremy. **Horseback Riding.** Crestwood House, 1992.

Greenspan, Bud. **100 Greatest Moments in Olympic History.** General Publishing, 1995.

Kidd, Jane. **A World of Horses.** Howell Book House, 1997.

Kristy, Davida. **Coubertin's Olympics: How the Games Began.** Lerner Publications, 1995.

Perry, Philippa. **Olympic Gold.** World Book, 1996.

Wallechinsky, David. **The Complete Book of the Summer Olympics.** Little, Brown & Co., 1996.

Organizations and Online Sites

American Horse Shows Association
4047 Iron Works Parkway
Lexington, KY 40511

The American Horse Shows Association supervises equestrian competitions in the United States.

Federation Equestre Internationale (FEI)
http://www.horsesport.org

This page can help you learn about the organization that supervises all international equestrian events.

International Olympic Committee (IOC)
http://www.olympic.org

Find out about the organization that runs all Olympic Games.

New Rider
http://www.newrider.com

A British horseback riding site that provides information on how to start, what to wear, where to go for lessons, how to get on a horse, and much more.

United States Equestrian Team
Pottersville Road
Gladstone, NJ 07934

The U.S. Equestrian Team represents the United States in international equestrian sports.

United States Olympic Committee (USOC)
Olympic House
One Olympic Plaza
Colorado Springs, CO 80909-5760

The United States Olympic Committee supervises Olympic activity for the United States.

Important Words

chariot two-wheeled horse-drawn car of ancient times

combined driving event in which the horse pulls its driver in a cart or carriage

endurance riding event in which horses and riders run over very long trails

equestrian events sports that take place on horseback

faults penalty points added to the score of a horse and rider

reining event that shows the athletic abilities of ranch horses

reins leather straps attached to the horse's mouth and used to help tell a horse what to do

saddle leather seat strapped to the horse's back

veterinarians doctors for horses and other animals

Index

Meet the Author

Bob Knotts is the author of five True Books on Summer Olympic sports. He also writes for national magazines, including *Sports Illustrated*, *Reader's Digest*, *Family Circle*, *Travel & Leisure*, and *USA Weekend*. He has worked as a newspaper reporter as well as in radio and television. He has been nominated twice for the Pulitzer Prize. Mr. Knotts resides with his wife, Jill, at their home near Fort Lauderdale, Florida.